WHERE'S WALLY?
THROUGH HISTORY
MARTIN HANDFORD

WALKER BOOKS
AND SUBSIDIARIES
LONDON · BOSTON · SYDNEY · AUCKLAND

HELLO, HISTORY-LOVERS!

HAVE YOU EVER WANTED TO TRAVEL INTO THE PAST AND DISCOVER WHAT THE WORLD WAS LIKE IN TIMES GONE BY? WELL, NOW IS YOUR CHANCE! HOP IN A TIME MACHINE AND DALLY WITH DINOSAURS, ROAM AMONGST THE ROMANS, JOIN THE GOLD RUSH IN THE WILD WEST AND MUCH, MUCH MORE!

CAN YOU ALSO FIND THIS HIDDEN HISTORY BOOK? IT ONLY APPEARS ONCE:

YOU CAN SPOT ME AND LOTS OF OTHER THINGS TO SEARCH FOR AS YOU WHIZZ THROUGH EVERY AGE, TOO. READY? IT'S TIME TO GO!

Wally

INVENTION O'CLOCK

First, you need to design your very own amazing time machine to travel back into the past! Be as creative as you like and add labels to show how everything works!

✏ Draw your time machine here!

A TICK-TOCK PASTIME

Now, whizz through these corridors of time.
Study the doors and keys as you pass them by,
then turn the page and test your memory.

TICK-TOCK MEMORY GAME

Can you remember which key goes above which door?
Draw a line from each key to the door it opens.

THROUGH THE KEYHOLE GAME

Take your time to peek through these keyholes.
Then turn back the page and find each section in the scene.

6

DINO-BALL

ROAR! We've arrived back when dinosaurs roamed the earth! Can you work out which rock comes next in these four sequences? Draw the size of the rock first, then colour it in.

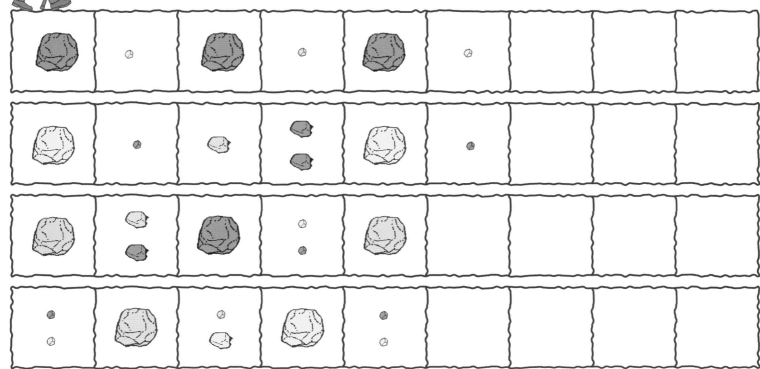

GAME 1

GAME 2

GAME 3

GAME 4

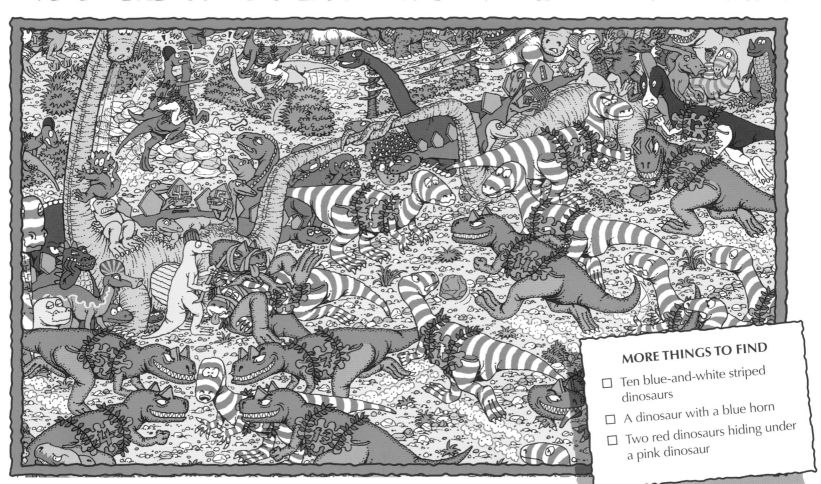

MORE THINGS TO FIND

☐ Ten blue-and-white striped dinosaurs

☐ A dinosaur with a blue horn

☐ Two red dinosaurs hiding under a pink dinosaur

FACTOSAURUS

Quiz time! Do you know your Diplodocuses from your Europasauruses? Test your knowledge below!

1. The word dinosaur means 'terrible lizard'.

2. A dinosaur scientist is called a dinotologist.

3. Dinosaurs laid eggs.

4. This anagram spells a dinosaur's name: RETTSRIPOCA

5. A Tyrannosaurus' bite was roughly three times stronger than that of a lion.

6. The Ankylosaurus had a club tail.

7. The dinosaur with the longest name is called a Micropachycephalosaurus.

8. A Pterodactyl had three wings.

9. A Brachiosaurus had a very short neck.

10. The dinosaurs lived until 65 thousand years ago.

Use the Internet or an encyclopaedia to help you, and look up more fun facts about dinosaurs.

DID YOU KNOW?

There was a dinosaur similar to a dog! It is called Cynognathus (sy-nog-nay-thus) and was a hairy mammal-like animal with dog-like teeth. Woof claims that his great-great-great grandfather was one (calculated in dog years, of course)!

ONE MORE THING

What is the name of the dinosaur whose skeleton is in this picture? *Clue: it begins with the letter 'S'.*

STONE AGE WORD WHEEL

Use the clues to help you find five words using three or more letters in the word wheel. Each answer must contain the letter O only once.

CLUES

1. It's as hard as rock
2. Woof's favourite thing
3. Used to sniff
4. Heads, shoulders, knees and...
5. Woof is one of these

2.

3.

4.

5.

1.

MORE THINGS TO DO
See how many other words you can make using the word wheel.

PYRAMID PUZZLE

Now, to Ancient Egypt! Search for the words at the bottom of this page in the pyramid puzzle. The words go up, down, forwards and backwards!

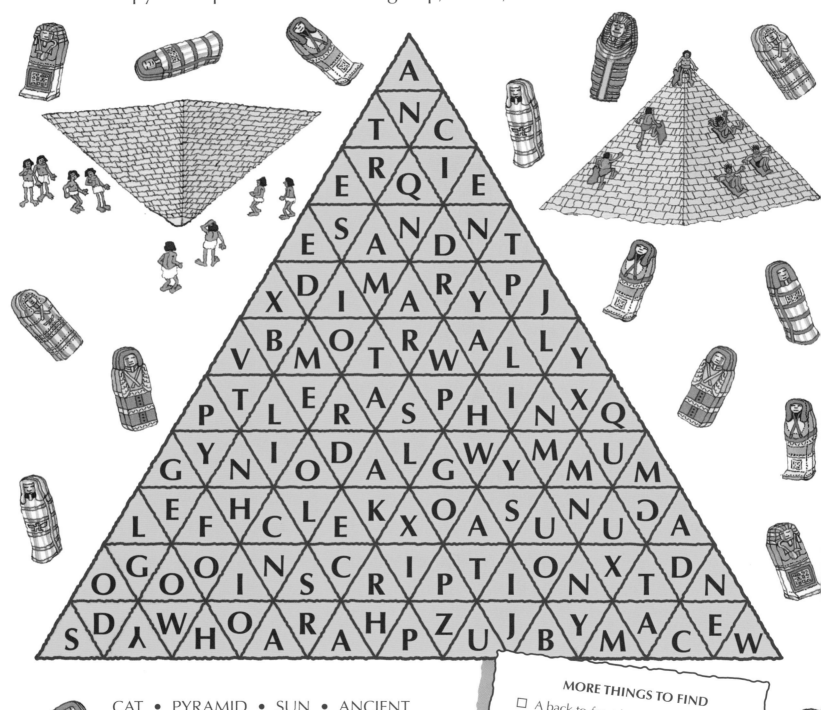

CAT • PYRAMID • SUN • ANCIENT
DESERT • WALLY • GODS • SAND
MUMMY • NILE • GOAT • PHARAOH
INSCRIPTION • TOMB • SPHINX • EGYPT

MORE THINGS TO FIND
☐ A back-to-front letter
☐ An upside-down letter
☐ The names of two of Wally's friends
(clue: see the start of the book!)

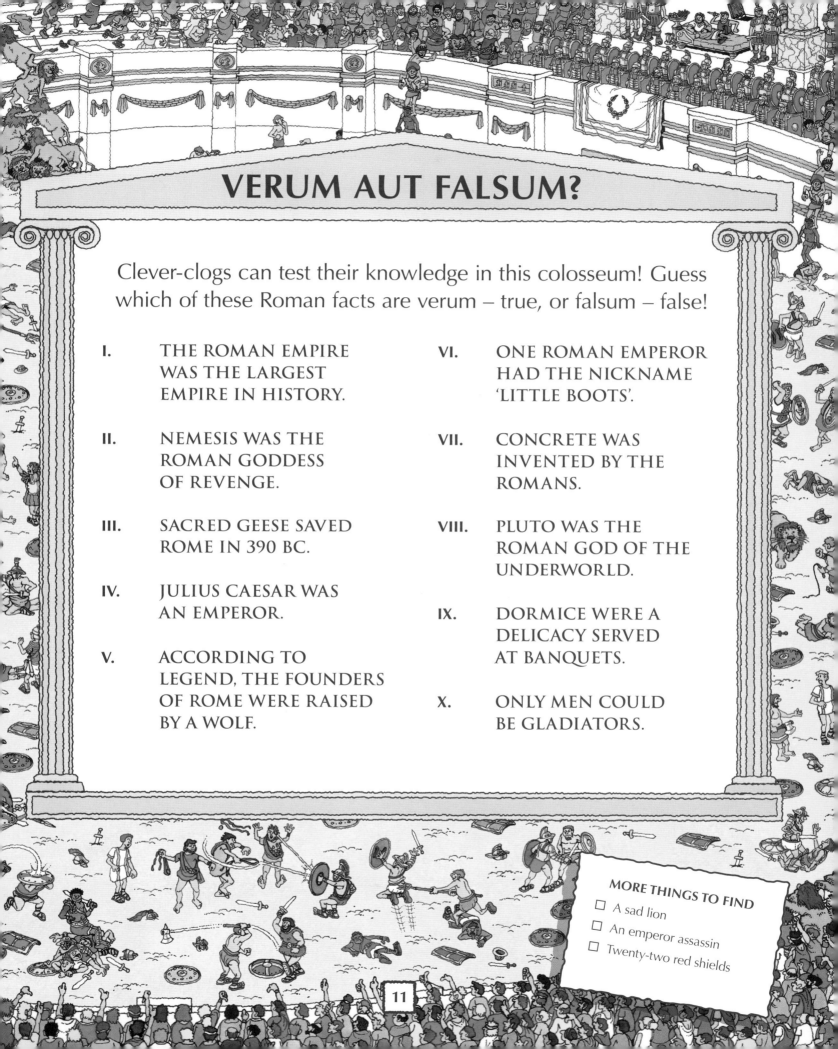

VERUM AUT FALSUM?

Clever-clogs can test their knowledge in this colosseum! Guess which of these Roman facts are verum – true, or falsum – false!

I. THE ROMAN EMPIRE WAS THE LARGEST EMPIRE IN HISTORY.

II. NEMESIS WAS THE ROMAN GODDESS OF REVENGE.

III. SACRED GEESE SAVED ROME IN 390 BC.

IV. JULIUS CAESAR WAS AN EMPEROR.

V. ACCORDING TO LEGEND, THE FOUNDERS OF ROME WERE RAISED BY A WOLF.

VI. ONE ROMAN EMPEROR HAD THE NICKNAME 'LITTLE BOOTS'.

VII. CONCRETE WAS INVENTED BY THE ROMANS.

VIII. PLUTO WAS THE ROMAN GOD OF THE UNDERWORLD.

IX. DORMICE WERE A DELICACY SERVED AT BANQUETS.

X. ONLY MEN COULD BE GLADIATORS.

MORE THINGS TO FIND
- ☐ A sad lion
- ☐ An emperor assassin
- ☐ Twenty-two red shields

FANT-AZTEC ART

The Aztecs made many amazing masks. Copy and colour in these designs then create your own in the empty space provided.

MORE THINGS TO FIND

☐ Two exhausted ball game players
☐ Five red feathers in headbands
☐ A person wearing a red nose
☐ A man wearing clown shoes

BATTLE OF THE FLAGS

This historical battleground is filled with bizarre banners! Find these funny flag faces in the scene below.

MORE THINGS TO FIND

☐ Two snakes

☐ A game of noughts and crosses

☐ Ten milk bottles

YE OLDE MARKET

It's a busy, bustling day in the Middle Ages. See if you can spot these colourful characters in the scene.

MORE THINGS TO FIND

- ☐ A back-to-front knight
- ☐ A juggling jester
- ☐ A band of minstrels
- ☐ An angry fish

WORD CASTLE

Find the words at the bottom of this page in the three-letter bricks of this castle. A word can read across more than one brick.

```
R O F       A Q U E E N       A X E
M X A       J O P W W O       W G R
L W A   D R A W   B R I   D G E H   L D R A
O A R   M O U R   E K R   C A T A   P U L T
N T P   C A S T   L E L Q   P U F M   P X E
W Q L   E U H E   L M E T   A B A T   T L E
M O A   T H Y K   W S E M   I U L E   I A F
D G E   M I L A   I N S I   S W O R   D W R
A R R   O W H R   E E A K   L K C E   T L H
H F M   A R A W   N P M T   L H F L   A G T
W K I   N G O H   Y O E A   B O S P   P C G
```

MORE THINGS TO DO

Work out the two magic words that can open the castle drawbridge. Then find it hidden in the word castle!

Clue: the letters go up, across and down.

O _ _ _ _ / _ _ S _ _ E

16

WORDS TO FIND

ARMOUR
SWORD
MOAT
ARROW
CASTLE
DRAWBRIDGE

CATAPULT
KING
QUEEN
HELMET
AXE
BATTLE

MUDDLED MUSKETEERS

Complete this jigsaw to make sense of the swashbuckling chaos!
If you can, try scanning the page and cutting out the pieces to
make the real thing. But be warned, there's a rogue piece!

MORE THINGS TO FIND

- ☐ A dizzy musketeer
- ☐ A chequered flag
- ☐ Six musketeers wearing blue crested tunics
- ☐ A musketeer dog statue
- ☐ A green sedan chair

WILD, WILD WORDS!

Yee-haw! The answers to this crossword puzzle are set in the wild, wild west.

Across

1. A large farm used to keep animals (5 letters)

3. The seat placed on a horse's back (6 letters)

4. Vessel with handle used to carry water (6 letters)

6. Someone who bends metal and mends horseshoes (10 letters)

9. The opposite to cold (3 letters)

10. A tool used to dig. Pick... (3 letters)

11. Midday (4 letters)

Down

1. To steal (3 letters)

2. Money offered on a poster for a wanted person (6 letters)

3. A rush of startled animals (8 letters)

5. A green plant with spikes (6 letters)

7. A looped rope used to catch horses (5 letters)

8. A mode of transport with carriages (5 letters)

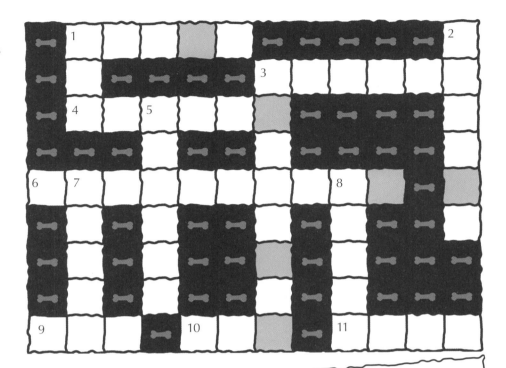

MORE THINGS TO DO

There are six letters in grey squares in the crossword puzzle. Can you unscramble the anagram to spell out grid coordinates and find where Woof has buried some gold coins on the next page? The answer will be a letter and a number spelt in letters.

___ / ___ ___ ___ ___

GOLD MINE

Dig for gold hidden in this grid! Fill in the coordinates for the items at the bottom of this page to mark where it's buried.

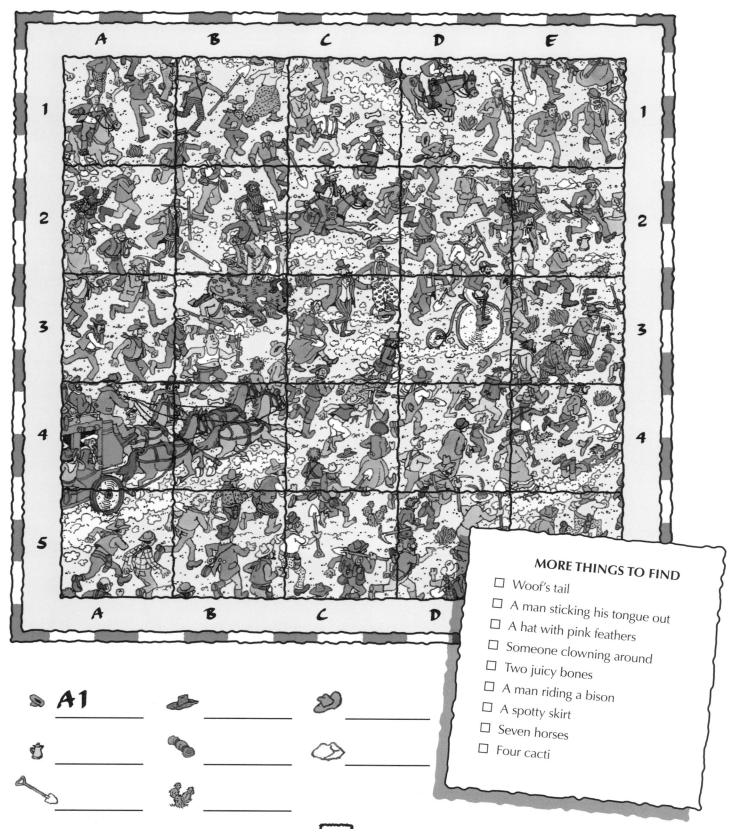

MORE THINGS TO FIND

- ☐ Woof's tail
- ☐ A man sticking his tongue out
- ☐ A hat with pink feathers
- ☐ Someone clowning around
- ☐ Two juicy bones
- ☐ A man riding a bison
- ☐ A spotty skirt
- ☐ Seven horses
- ☐ Four cacti

A1

MIX-UP MADNESS

What a muddle! Match the top and bottom halves of these historical figures. Watch out for Wally and his friends, too!

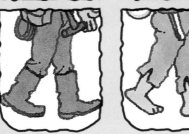

MORE THINGS TO DO

- Draw your own fantasy characters in the two blank boxes!
- Give some of the mixed-up characters combination names, like "Vikingator" (viking + gladiator)!

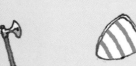

BLAST TO THE FUTURE

Through history and into outer space! Colour in this rocket filled with futuristic friends and write which planet you're going to on the line below!

Planet ....

WOW, WHAT A BLAST WE'VE HAD IN THE PAST! WHICH ERA WAS YOUR FAVOURITE? WOULD YOU RATHER LIVE BACK IN TIME OR IN THE FUTURE? YOU MAY HAVE ALREADY FOUND MY HIDDEN HISTORY BOOK, BUT DID YOU SEE THIS VERY FUTURISTIC ROBOT THAT CRASH-LANDED INTO ANOTHER AGE?

TICK TOCK!

Wally

Put your time machine into reverse! Look through the pages again to find these hard-to-spot items!

A CHECKLIST THROUGH HISTORY

- Two people colliding with a cactus
- A man behind bars
- A donkey carrying a heavy load
- A person riding a penny farthing bicycle
- A man with a long white beard
- An extravagant birthday cake
- A lion spectator
- A photographer
- Three cave-dwellers swinging
- A person playing a French horn
- A musketeer statue
- Two women with sliced hats
- A pink parasol
- Three escaped convicts
- A blue feather headband
- A man with ticklish feet
- An egg timer
- A fire-breathing gargoyle

HERE ARE SOME ANSWERS TO THE HARDEST PUZZLES. DON'T GIVE UP ON THE OTHERS – WHY NOT ASK YOUR FRIENDS TO HELP?

P. 7 DINO-BALL

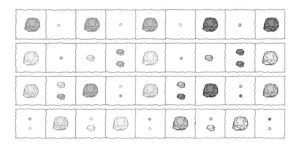

P. 8 FACTOSAURUS

1. True; 2. False: A dinosaur scientist is called a paleontologist; 3. True; 4. True: TRICERATOPS; 5. True; 6. True; 7. True; 8. False: It had two wings; 9. False: It had a very long neck; 10. False: Dinosaurs actually lived until sixty-five million years ago. Wow!

P. 9 STONE AGE WORD WHEEL

It's as hard as rock – stone; *Woof's favourite thing* – bone; *Used to sniff* – nose; *Heads, shoulders, knees and* – toes; *Woof is one of these* – dog

P. 10 PYRAMID PUZZLE

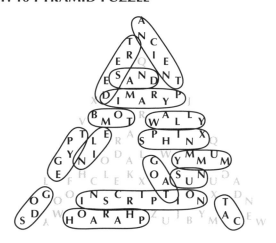

P. 11 VERUM AUT FALSUM

1. False: The British Empire was the largest in history and at its peak covered a quarter of the globe; 2. True; 3. True; 4. False: Julius Caesar was not an emperor but his adopted son Caesar Augustus was the first Roman emperor; 5. True; 6. True; 7. True; 8. True; 9. True; 10. False: There were female gladiators called gladiatrix. They would fight each other and wild animals.

P. 16 WORD CASTLE

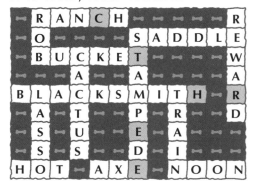

MORE THINGS TO DO: open sesame

P. 19 WILD, WILD WORDS!

MORE THINGS TO DO: c / three

P. 21 MIX-UP MADNESS

First published 2022 by Walker Books Ltd, 87 Vauxhall Walk, London SE11 5HJ • 2 4 6 8 10 9 7 5 3 • © 1987–2022 Martin Handford • The right of Martin Handford to be identified as author/illustrator of this work has been asserted by him in accordance with the Copyright, Designs and Patents Act 1988. • This book has been typeset in Wallyfont and Optima • Printed in China • All rights reserved. • British Library Cataloguing in Publication Data: a catalogue record for this book is available from the British Library. • ISBN 978-1-5295-0315-9 • www.walker.co.uk